Bannockburn School Dist. 106
2165 Telegraph Road
Bannockburn, Illinois 60015

DATE DUE

FOLLETT

First Facts®

Our Physical World

Matter

Bannockburn School Dist. 106
2165 Telegraph Road
Bannockburn, Illinois 60015

by Christine Webster

Consultant:
Philip W. Hammer, PhD
Vice President, The Franklin Center
The Franklin Institute
Philadelphia, Pennsylvania

Capstone
press®

Mankato, Minnesota

First Facts is published by Capstone Press,
151 Good Counsel Drive, P.O. Box 669, Mankato, Minnesota 56002.
www.capstonepress.com

092009
5613R

Library of Congress Cataloging-in-Publication Data
Webster, Christine.
    Matter / by Christine Webster.
    p. cm.—(First facts. Our physical world)
    Includes bibliographical references and index.
    Contents: Matter—Solids—Liquids—Gases—Changing matter—Using matter—Jacques
Charles—Matter safety—Amazing but true!—Hands on: gas pressure.
    ISBN-13: 978-0-7368-2617-4 (hardcover)
    ISBN-10: 0-7368-2617-3 (hardcover)
    ISBN-13: 978-0-7368-5157-2 (softcover pbk.)
    ISBN-10: 0-7368-5157-7 (softcover pbk.)
    1. Matter—Juvenile literature. [1. Matter.] I. Title. II. Series.
QC173.36.W33 2005
530—dc22   2003026411

Summary: Introduces matter and provides instructions for an activity to demonstrate
    some of its characteristics.

Editorial Credits
Christopher Harbo, editor; Linda Clavel, series designer; Molly Nei, book designer;
    Scott Thoms, photo researcher; Eric Kudalis, product planning editor

Photo Credits
Capstone Press/Gary Sundermeyer, cover, 6, 8–9, 10–11, 12–13, 14, 15, 19
Corbis, 20; Bettmann, 16; Glenn McLaughlin, 5; Owaki-Kulla, 7

Table of Contents

Matter

Matter is everywhere. Matter is anything that takes up space and has **mass**. Mass is the amount of material in an object. Matter has three forms. These forms are **solid**, **liquid**, and **gas**. A wooden dock, pond water, and air are all matter.

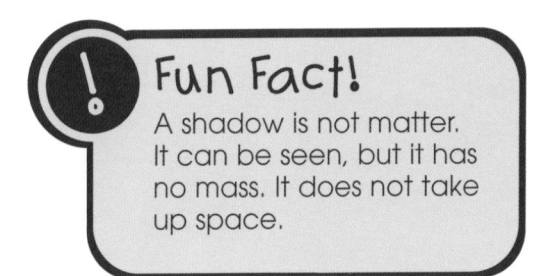

Fun Fact!
A shadow is not matter. It can be seen, but it has no mass. It does not take up space.

Solids

A solid is matter that holds its own shape. Solids can be hard or soft. Metal, wood, and clay are solids.

Energy can be used to change the shape of solids. A person uses heat and a hammer to pound iron into a new shape.

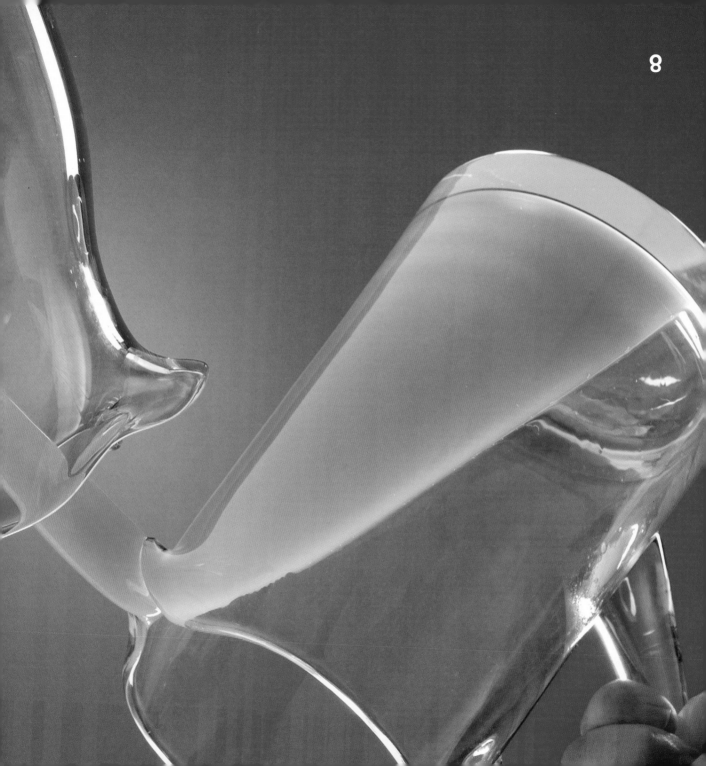

Liquids

Liquids have no shape of their own. They flow freely when they are poured. Liquids also take the shape of what holds them. Orange juice poured into a pitcher takes the shape of the pitcher.

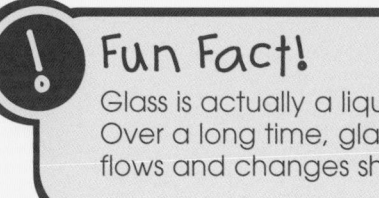

Fun Fact!
Glass is actually a liquid. Over a long time, glass flows and changes shape.

Gases

Gases have no shape. Most gases can't be seen. The air we breathe is a gas. Gases spread out and fill the total area they are in. A balloon **expands** when it is filled with air.

Changing Matter

Matter changes when heated or cooled. Ice changes from a solid to a liquid when heated. Water changes from a liquid to a gas when boiled. The gas turns back into liquid water when it touches something cooler.

Using Matter

People use matter all the time. A cup is solid matter. It holds drinks. A drink, such as soda, is liquid matter.

The bubbles in soda are **carbon dioxide** gas. People swallow this gas when they drink soda. When they burp, the carbon dioxide rises out of their stomachs.

Jacques Charles

Jacques Charles was a French scientist in the 1700s. He studied gases. In 1787, he learned that gases expand when they are heated. This discovery became the idea for Charles' Law. It states that the **volume** of any gas increases as its temperature increases.

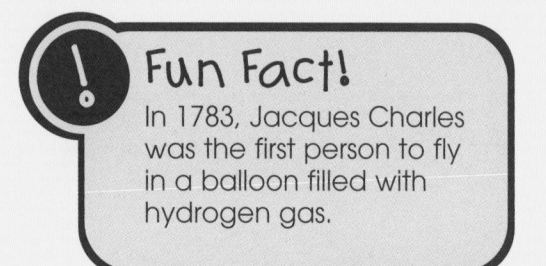

Fun Fact!

In 1783, Jacques Charles was the first person to fly in a balloon filled with hydrogen gas.

Matter Safety

Matter can be dangerous when it changes. Boiling changes water from a liquid to a gas. The steam from boiling water is very hot. It can burn a person's skin. Always ask an adult to help when boiling water.

19

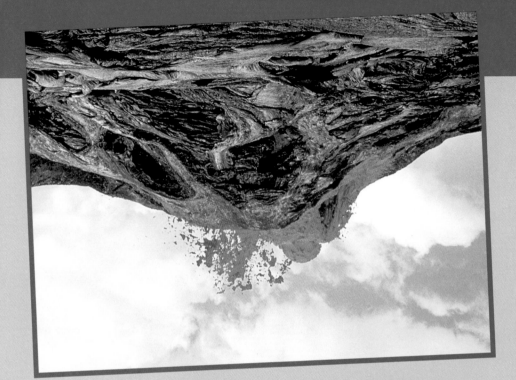

Inside earth is hot liquid rock. When a volcano erupts, liquid rock breaks through earth's surface. The liquid rock cools and becomes solid. The Hawaiian Islands formed when rock changed from a liquid to a solid.

Amazing but True!

Hands On: Gas Pressure

Gases expand to fill the space of what holds them. Try this experiment to see how expanding gas can inflate a balloon.

What You Need

funnel
3 teaspoons (15 mL) baking soda
balloon
2 tablespoons (30 mL) white vinegar
plastic soda bottle

What You Do

1. Use a funnel to pour baking soda into the balloon. Set aside.
2. Pour vinegar into the plastic bottle.
3. Holding the balloon upside down, stretch the opening of the balloon over the neck of the bottle. Do not let the baking soda fall into the bottle yet.
4. When the balloon is on the neck of the bottle, quickly lift the balloon up. Shake the balloon so all of the baking soda falls into the bottle. Watch what happens to the balloon.

Baking soda and vinegar have a chemical reaction when mixed. They give off carbon dioxide gas. The gas expands to inflate the balloon.

Glossary

carbon dioxide (KAR-buhn dye-OK-side)—a gas found naturally in the air; carbon dioxide has no smell or color.

energy (EN-ur-jee)—the ability to move things or do work

expand (ek-SPAND)—to increase in size

gas (GASS)—a substance that spreads to fill any space that holds it

liquid (LIK-wid)—a substance that takes the shape of its container

mass (MASS)—the amount of material in an object

solid (SOL-id)—a substance that holds its shape

volume (VOL-yuhm)—the amount of space taken up by an object

Read More

McLuskey, Krista. *The Science of Liquids and Solids.* Living Science. Milwaukee: Gareth Stevens, 2001.

Royston, Angela. *Solids, Liquids, and Gasses.* My World of Science. Chicago: Heinemann Library, 2002.

Internet Sites

FactHound offers a safe, fun way to find Internet sites related to this book. All of the sites on FactHound have been researched by our staff.

Here's how:
1. Visit *www.facthound.com*
2. Type in this special code **0736826173** for age-appropriate sites. Or enter a search word related to this book for a more general search.
3. Click on the **Fetch It** button.

FactHound will fetch the best sites for you!

Index